Contents

One, Two, Buckle My Shoe

*This is an action rhyme as well as a counting rhyme. Make the actions suggested by the words.
Here are some suggestions for the more tricky verses:*

A big fat hen: spread your arms out wide.
Maids a-courting: blow a kiss.
Maids in the kitchen: pretend to stir a bowl of cake-mixture.
Maids in waiting: pretend to be carrying a tray.
My plate's empty: rub your tummy to show you're full up.

One, two,
Buckle my shoe;

Three, four,
Knock at the door;

Five, six,
Pick up sticks;

Seven, eight,
Lay them straight;

A Macmillan Poetry Book

One, Two, BUCKLE My Shoe

ACTION and COUNTING Rhymes

Illustrations by Anna Currey

MACMILLAN CHILDREN'S BOOKS

Acknowledgements

The publishers wish to thank the following for permission to use copyright material:

Jack Prelutsky, 'Countdown' from *It's Halloween*, William Heinemann, by permission of Egmont Children's Books Ltd; **Clive Sansom**, 'The Postman', by permission of David Higham on behalf of the author.

Every effort has been made to trace the copyright holders but if any have been inadvertently overlooked the publishers will be pleased to make the necessary arrangement at the first opportunity.

First published in 1999 by Macmillan Children's Books
A division of Macmillan Publishers Limited
25 Eccleston Place, London SW1W 9NF
Basingstoke and Oxford
Associated companies throughout the world.

ISBN 0 333 78074 4

1 3 5 7 9 8 6 4 2

Printed in Belgium

Nine, ten,
A big fat hen;

Eleven, twelve,
Dig and delve;

Thirteen, fourteen,
Maids a-courting;

Fifteen, sixteen,
Maids in the kitchen;

Seventeen, eighteen,
Maids in waiting;

Nineteen, twenty,
My plate's empty.

Anon.

Ring-a-Ring o' Roses

All hold hands and skip round in a ring.
On the last line of each verse, all sit down on the ground.

Ring-a-ring o' roses,
  A pocket full of posies.
    A-tishoo! A-tishoo!
We all fall down.

Ring-a-ring o' roses,
A pocket full of posies.
One for you, and one for me,
And one for little Moses.
A-tishoo! A-tishoo! We all fall down.

Anon.

Teddy Bear

Do the same actions as teddy!

Teddy bear,
Teddy bear, touch your nose,
Teddy bear,
Teddy bear, touch your toes,
Teddy bear,
Teddy bear, touch the ground,
Teddy bear,
Teddy bear, turn around.

Teddy bear,
Teddy bear, climb the stairs,
Teddy bear,
Teddy bear, say your prayers,
Teddy bear,
Teddy bear, turn off the light,
Teddy bear,
Teddy bear, say good night!

Anon.

Peanut Butter and Jelly

Make the actions suggested by the words. Whenever you say "Peanut butter, peanut butter, jelly, jelly", clap or stamp in time to the words.

First you take the dough and knead it,
  knead it.
Peanut butter, peanut butter, jelly, jelly.
Pop it in the oven and bake it, bake it.
Peanut butter, peanut butter, jelly, jelly.
Then you take a knife and slice it,
  slice it.
Peanut butter, peanut butter, jelly, jelly.
Then you take the peanuts and crack them,
  crack them.
Peanut butter, peanut butter, jelly, jelly.
Put them on the floor and mash them,
  mash them.

Peanut butter, peanut butter, jelly, jelly.
Then you take a knife and spread it,
    spread it.
Peanut butter, peanut butter, jelly, jelly.
Next you take some grapes and squash them,
    squash them.
Peanut butter, peanut butter, jelly, jelly.
Glop it on the bread and smear it, smear it.
Peanut butter, peanut butter, jelly, jelly.
Then you take the sandwich and eat it,
    eat it.
Peanut butter, peanut butter, jelly, jelly.

Anon.

The Postman

Knock on the table or stamp on the floor in time to the words "Rat-a-tat-tat".

Rat-a-tat-tat, Rat-a-tat-tat,
   Rat-a-tat-tat tattoo!
That's the way the Postman goes,
   Rat-a-tat-tat tattoo!
Every morning at half-past eight
You hear a bang at the garden gate,
And Rat-a-tat-tat, Rat-a-tat-tat,
   Rat-a-tat-tat tattoo!

Clive Sansom

Countdown

There are ten ghosts in the pantry,
There are nine upon the stairs,
There are eight ghosts in the attic,
There are seven on the chairs,
There are six within the kitchen,
There are five along the hall,
There are four upon the ceiling,
There are three upon the wall,
There are two ghosts on the carpet,
Doing things that ghosts will do,
There is one ghost right behind me
Who is oh so quiet . . . BOO!

Jack Prelutsky

Oliver Twist

Do the actions the rhyme suggests.

Oliver-Oliver-Oliver Twist
Bet you a penny you can't do this:
Number one—touch your tongue.
Number two—touch your shoe.
Number three—touch your knee.
Number four—touch the floor.
Number five—stay alive.
Number six—wiggle your hips.
Number seven—jump to Heaven.
Number eight—bang the gate.
Number nine—walk the line.
Number ten—start again.

Anon.

Do Your Ears Hang Low?

Do the actions the rhyme suggests.

Do your ears hang low?
Do they wobble to and fro?
Can you tie them in a knot?
Can you tie them in a bow?
Can you throw them over your shoulder
Like a regimental soldier?
Do your ears hang low?

Anon.

Here is the Ostrich

Pretend to be each animal in the poem.

Here is the ostrich straight and tall,
Nodding his head above us all.

Here is the long snake on the ground,
    Wriggling on the stones around.

Here are the birds that fly so high,
Spreading their wings across the sky.

Here is the bushrat, furry and small,
Rolling himself into a ball.

Here is the spider scuttling round,
Treading so lightly on the ground.

Here are the children fast asleep,
And here at night the owls do peep.

Anon.

Five Little Pussy Cats

Five little pussy cats playing near the door;
    One ran and hid inside
    And then there were four.

Four little pussy cats underneath a tree;
    One heard a dog bark
    And then there were three.

Three little pussy cats thinking what to do;
   One saw a little bird
   And then there were two.

Two little pussy cats sitting in the sun;
   One ran to catch his tail
   And then there was one.

One little pussy cat looking for some fun;
   He saw a butterfly—
   And then there was none.

Anon.

Down in the Grass

Pretend your arm is the snake. You could rest your elbow on a table to do this. Make the snake's head by touching your fingertip with your thumb.

Down in the grass, curled up in a heap,
Lies a big snake, fast asleep.
When he hears the grasses blow,
He moves his body to and fro.
Up and down and in and out,
See him slowly move about!
Now his jaws are open, so—
Snap! He's caught my finger! Oh!

Anon.

18

The Elephant

An elephant goes like this and that.

Pat your knees.

He's terrible big,

Stretch your arms up high.

And he's terrible fat.

Stretch your arms out wide.

He has no fingers,

Wriggle your fingers.

And he has no toes,

Touch your toes.

But goodness gracious, what a nose!

Pretend your arm is an elephant's trunk.

Anon.

I Love Sixpence

I love sixpence, jolly little sixpence,
  I love sixpence better than my life;
I spent a penny of it, I lent a penny of it,
  And I took fourpence home to my wife.

Oh, my little fourpence, jolly little fourpence,
  I love fourpence better than my life;
I spent a penny of it, I lent a penny of it,
  And I took twopence home to my wife.

Oh, my little twopence, jolly little twopence,
  I love twopence better than my life;
I spent a penny of it, I lent a penny of it,
  And I took nothing home to my wife.

Oh, my little nothing, jolly little nothing,
  What will nothing buy for my wife?
I have nothing, I spend nothing,
  I love nothing better than my wife.

Anon.

Oh Where, Oh Where?

Pretend to be looking high and low for your little dog.
Mime his short ears and long tail, too.

Oh where, oh where has my little dog gone?
  Oh where, oh where can he be?
With his ears cut short and his tail cut long,
  Oh where, oh where is he?

Anon.

Two Little Dicky Birds

Two little dicky birds
Sitting on a wall,

Use your two index fingers to be Peter and Paul.

One named Peter,

Wiggle the finger which is Peter.

One named Paul.

Wiggle the finger which is Paul.

Fly away Peter,

Put the finger which is Peter behind your back.

Fly away Paul;

Put the finger which is Paul behind your back.

Come back Peter,
Come back Paul.

Bring each finger back in front of you.

Anon.

Incey Wincey Spider

Incey Wincey spider
Climbing up the spout;

Use all your fingers to show how the spider climbs up.

Down came the rain
And washed the spider out:

Wriggle your fingers down to show the rain.

Out came the sun
And dried up all the rain;

Sweep your hands up and bring them out and down.

Incey Wincey spider
Climbing up again.

Do the same as for the first line.

Anon.

One, Two, Three, Four

One, two, three, four,
Mary at the cottage door,
Five, six, seven, eight,
Eating cherries off a plate.

Anon.

One, Two, Three, Four, Five

One, two, three, four, five,
Once I caught a fish alive,
Six, seven, eight, nine, ten,
Then I let it go again.
Why did you let it go?
Because it bit my finger so.
Which finger did it bite?
This little finger on the right.

Anon.

Bow-Wow, Says the Dog

Make all the animal noises.

Bow-wow, says the dog,
Mew, mew, says the cat,
Grunt, grunt, goes the hog,
And squeak goes the rat.
Tu-whu, says the owl,
Caw, caw, says the crow,
Quack, quack, says the duck,
And what cuckoos say you know.

Anon.

Old Noah's Ark

Old Noah once he built an ark,
And patched it up with hickory bark.
He anchored it to a great big rock,
And then he began to load his stock.
The animals went in one by one,
The elephant chewing a carroway bun.
The animals went in two by two,
The crocodile and the kangaroo.

The animals went in three by three,
The tall giraffe and the tiny flea.
The animals went in four by four,
The hippopotamus stuck in the door.
The animals went in five by five,
The bees mistook the bear for a hive.
The animals went in six by six,
The monkey was up to his usual tricks.

The animals went in seven by seven,
Said the ant to the elephant,
 "Who're ye shov'n?"
The animals went in eight by eight,
Some were early and some were late.
The animals went in nine by nine,
They all formed fours and marched
 in a line.
The animals went in ten by ten,
If you want any more, you can
 read it again.

Anon.

28

Here We Go Round the Mulberry Bush

Join hands and skip round in a circle on the first verse, then repeat this verse as a chorus after verses two and three. Mime the actions in verses two and three.

Here we go round the mulberry bush,
The mulberry bush, the mulberry bush,
Here we go round the mulberry bush,
On a cold and frosty morning.

This is the way we wash our hands,
Wash our hands, wash our hands,
This is the way we wash our hands,
On a cold and frosty morning.

This is the way we wash our clothes,
Wash our clothes, wash our clothes,
This is the way we wash our clothes,
On a cold and frosty morning.

Anon.

Oranges and Lemons

Two children form an arch with their arms, and decide secretly which of them is going to be "oranges" and which is going to be "lemons". Then all the other children file under the arch, singing the rhyme to the traditional tune. On the last line of the song, the children forming the arch bring their arms up and down on each word, "trapping" each of the children as they file under. Whoever is "trapped" on the very last word of the song has to whisper either "oranges" or "lemons" and then go and stand behind whichever child they have chosen, so that gradually two lines of children form on either side of the arch. When all the children have been "trapped", the two sides can have a tug-of-war.

Gay go up and gay go down,
To ring the bells of London town.

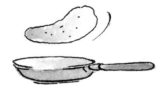

Oranges and lemons,
Say the bells of St Clement's.

Pancakes and fritters,
Say the bells of St Peter's.

Two sticks and an apple,
Say the bells at Whitechapel.

Old Father Baldpate,
Say the slow bells at Aldgate.

Pokers and tongs,
Say the bells at St John's.

Kettles and pans,
Say the bells at St Ann's.

You owe me five farthings,
Say the bells at St Martin's.

When will you pay me,
Say the bells at Old Bailey.

When I grow rich,
Say the bells at Shoreditch.

Pray when will that be?
Say the bells of Stepney.

I'm sure I don't know,
Says the great bell at Bow.

Here comes a candle to light you to bed,
And here comes a chopper to chop off
   your head.
Last, last, last, last, last man's head.

Anon.